Grave of the Last Saxon by William Lisle Bowles

William Lisle Bowles was born on 24th September 1762 at King's Sutton in Northamptonshire.

His great-grandfather, grandfather and his father, William Thomas Bowles, had all been parish priests and inevitably Bowles would join their line.

In 1789 Bowles published, a small quarto volume, Fourteen Sonnets, which was received with extraordinary praise, not only by the general public, but by such revered poets as Samuel Taylor Coleridge and Wordsworth.

After receiving his degree at Oxford, Bowles now began his career in service to the Church of England.

His years of service perhaps diminished both his stature as a poet and certainly the way he was viewed. For much of his career Bowles was seen as rather soft when set against his contemporaries but in the end his ability as a poet was enshrined, after a long and ferocious attack against him, by the principles he so eloquently wrote about and adhered too.

In personality and nature Bowles was said to be an amiable, absent-minded, but rather eccentric man. His poems speak warmly of a refinement of feeling, tenderness, and pensive thought, but are lacking in power and passion. But that should not diminish their value or appreciation to us.

Bowles maintained that images drawn from nature are poetically finer than those drawn from art; and that in the highest kinds of poetry the themes or passions handled should be of the general or elemental kind, and not the transient manners of any society.

As well as his poetry Bowles was also responsible for writing a Life of Bishop Ken (in two volumes, 1830–1831), Coombe Ellen and St. Michael's Mount (1798), The Battle of the Nile (1799), and The Sorrows of Switzerland (1801).

William Lisle Bowles died on April 7th, 1850 at the age of 87.

Index of Contents

INTRODUCTION

The circumstance of the late critical controversy with Lord Byron having recalled my attention to a poem, sketched some years ago, on a subject of national history, I have been induced to revise and correct, and now venture to offer it to the public.

The subject, though taken from an early period of our history, is, so far as relates to the grave of Harold, purely imaginary, as are all the characters, except those of the Conqueror, and of Edgar Atheling. History, I think, justifies me in representing William as acting constantly under strong religious impressions. A few circumstances in his life will clearly show this. When Harold was with him in Normandy, he took an oath of him on two altars, within which were concealed miraculous relics. His banner was sent from Rome, consecrated by the Pope, for the especial purpose of the invasion of England. Without adverting to the night spent in prayer before the battle of Hastings, was not this impression more decidedly shown when he pitched his tent among the dead on that night, and vowed to build an abbey on the spot? The event of the battle was so much against all human probability, that his undertaking it, at the place and time, can only be reconciled by supposing that he acted under some extraordinary impression.

When the battle was gained, he knew not on what course to determine: instead of marching to London, he retired towards Dover. When he was met by the Kentish men, with green boughs, the quaint historian says, "He was daunted." These and many other incidental circumstances may occur to the reader.

In representing him, therefore, as under the control of superstitious impressions, I trust I have not transgressed, at least, poetical verisimilitude. An earthquake actually happened about the period at which the poem commences, followed by storms and inundations. Of these facts I have availed myself.

I fear the poem will be thought less interesting, from having nothing of love in it, except, in accordance with the received ideas of the gentleness of Atheling's character, I have made him not insensible to one of my imaginary females; and have, therefore, to mark his character, made him advert to the pastoral scenes of Scotland, where he had been a resident. There is a similarity between my "Monk," and "The Missionary," but their offices and the scenes are entirely different, and some degree of resemblance was unavoidable in characters of the same description.

Filial affection, love of our country, bravery, sternness (inflexible, except under religions fears); the loftier feelings of a desolate female, under want and affliction, with something of the wild prophetical cast; religious submission, and deep acquiescence in the will of God;—these passions are brought into action, around one centre, if I may use the word, THE GRAVE OF THE LAST SAXON.

That Harold's sons landed with a large fleet from Denmark, and were joined by an immense confederate army, in the third year of William's reign, is a well-known historical fact. That York was taken by the confederate army, and that all the Normans, except Sir William Malet, and his family, were killed, is also matter of record. That afterwards, the blow against William failing, the whole country, from the Humber to Tyne, from the east to the west, was depopulated by sword and famine, are facts which are also to be found in all historians.

Some slight anachronisms may I hope, be pardoned—if anachronisms they are—such as the year in which the Tower was built, etc.

The plan of the Poem will be found, I trust, simple and coherent, the characters sufficiently marked and contrasted, and the whole conducive, however deficient in other respects, to the excitement of virtuous sympathy, and subservient to that which alone can give dignity to poetry—the cause of moral and religious truth.

FOOTNOTES:

Footnote : See the picture in Stodhard's Travels.

Footnote : Vide Drake's History of York, and Turner's History of England.

THE GRAVE OF THE LAST SAXON

INTRODUCTORY CANTO

Subject—Grave and children of Harold—Confederate army of Danes, Scottish, and English arrived in the Humber the third year of the Conqueror, and marching to York

"Know ye the land where the bright orange glows!"
Oh! rather know ye not the land, beloved
Of Liberty, where your brave fathers bled!
The land of the white cliffs, where every cot
Whose smoke goes up in the clear morning sky,
On the green hamlet's edge, stands as secure
As the proud Norman castle's bannered keep!
Oh! shall the poet paint a land of slaves,
(Albeit, that the richest colours warm
His tablet, glowing from the master's hand,)
And thee forget, his country—thee, his home!
Fair Italy! thy hills and olive-groves
A lovelier light empurples, or when morn
Streams o'er the cloudless van of Apennine,
Or more majestic eve, on the wide scene
Of columns, temples, arches, and aqueducts,
Sits, like reposing Glory, and collects
Her richest radiance at that parting hour;
While distant domes, touched by her hand, shine out
More solemnly, 'mid the gray monuments
That strew the illustrious plain; yet say, can these,
Even when their pomp is proudest, and the sun
Sinks o'er the ruins of immortal Rome,
A holy interest wake, intense as that
Which visits his full heart, who, severed long,
And home returning, sees once more the light
Shine on the land where his forefathers sleep;

Sees its white cliffs at distance, and exclaims:
There I was born, and there my bones shall rest!
Then, oh! ye bright pavilions of the East,
Ye blue Italian skies, and summer seas,
By marble cliffs high-bounded, throwing far
A gray illumination through the haze
Of orient morning; ye, Etruscan shades,
Where Pan's own pines o'er Valambrosa wave;
Scenes where old Tiber, for the mighty dead
As mourning, heavily rolls; or Anio
Flings its white foam; or lucid Arno steals
On gently through the plains of Tuscany;
Be ye the impassioned themes of other song.
Nor mine, thou wondrous Western World, to call
The thunder of thy cataracts, or paint
The mountains and the vast volcano range
Of Cordilleras, high above the stir
Of human things; lifting to middle air
Their snows in everlasting solitude;
Upon whose nether crags the vulture, lord
Of summits inaccessible, looks down,
Unhearing, when the thunder dies below!
Nor, 'midst the irriguous valleys of the south,
Where Chili spreads her green lap to the sea,
Now pause I to admire the bright blue bird,
Brightest and least of all its kind, that spins
Its twinkling flight, still humming o'er the flowers,
Like a gem of flitting light!
To these adieu!
Yet ere thy melodies, my harp, are mute
For ever, whilst the stealing day goes out
With slow-declining pace, I would essay
One patriot theme, one ancient British song:
So might I fondly dream, when the cold turf
Is heaped above my head, and carping tongues
Have ceased, some tones, Old England, thy green hills
Might then remember.

Time has reft the shrine
Where the last Saxon, canonized, lay,
And every trace has vanished, like the light
That from the high-arched eastern window fell,
With broken sunshine on his marble tomb—
So have they passed; and silent are the choirs,
That to his spirit sang eternal rest;
And scattered are his bones who raised those walls,
Where, from the field of blood slowly conveyed,
His mangled corse, with torch and orison,

Before the altar, and in holy earth,
Was laid! Yet oft I muse upon the theme;
And now, whilst solemn the slow curfew tolls,
Years and dim centuries seem to unfold
Their shroud, as at the summons; and I think
How sad that sound on every English heart
Smote, when along those darkening vales, where Lea
Beneath the woods of Waltham winds, it broke
First on the silence of the night, far heard
Through the deep forest! Phantoms of the past,
Ye gather round me! Voices of the dead,
Ye come by fits! And now I hear, far off,
Faint Eleesons swell, whilst to the fane
The long procession, and the pomp of death,
Moves visible; and now one voice is heard
From a vast multitude, Harold, farewell!
Farewell, and rest in peace! That sable car
Bears the last Saxon to his grave; the last
From Hengist, of the long illustrious line
That swayed the English sceptre. Hark! a cry!
'Tis from his mother, who, with frantic mien,
Follows the bier: with manly look composed,
Godwin, his eldest-born, and Adela,
Her head declined, her hand upon her brow
Beneath the veil, supported by his arm,
Sorrowing succeed! Lo! pensive Edmund there
Leads Wolfe, the least and youngest, by the hand!
Brothers and sisters, silent and in tears,
Follow their father to the dust, beneath
Whose eye they grew. Last and alone, behold,
Magnus, subduing the deep sigh, with brow
Of sterner acquiescence. Slowly pace
The sad remains of England's chivalry,
The few whom Hastings' field of carnage spared,
To follow their slain monarch's hearse this night,
Whose corse is borne beneath the escutcheoned pall,
To rest in Waltham Abbey. So the train,
Imagination thus embodies it,
Moves onward to the abbey's western porch,
Whose windows and retiring aisles reflect
The long funereal lights. Twelve stoled monks,
Each with a torch, and pacing, two and two,
Along the pillared nave, with crucifix
Aloft, begin the supplicating chant,
Intoning "Miserere Domine."
Now the stone coffins in the earth are laid
Of Harold, and of Leofrine, and Girth,
Brave brethren slain in one disastrous day.

And hark! again the monks and choristers
Sing, pacing round the grave-stone, "Requiem
Eternamdonaiis." To his grave
So was King Harold borne, within those walls
His bounty raised: his children knelt and wept,
Then slow departed, never in this world,
Perhaps, to meet again. But who is she,
Her dark hair streaming on her brow, her eye
Wild, and her breast deep-heaving? She beheld
At distance the due rites, nor wept, nor spake,
And now is gone!
Alas! from that sad hour,
By many fates, all who that hour had met
Were scattered. Godwin, Edmund, Adela,
Exiles in Denmark, there a refuge found
From England's stormy fortunes. Three long years
Have passed; again they tread their native land.
The Danish armament beneath the Spurn
Is anchored. Twenty thousand men at arms
Follow huge Waltheof, on his barbed steed,
His battle-axe hung at the saddle-bow;
Morcar and Edwin, English earls, are there,
With red-cross banner, and ten thousand men
From Ely and Northumberland; they raise
The death-song of defiance, and advance
With bows of steel. From Scotland's mountain-glens,
From sky-blue lochs, and the wild highland heaths,
From Lothian villages, along the banks
Of Forth, King Malcolm leads his clansmen bold,
And, dauntless as romantic, bids unfurl
The banner of St Andrew; by his side
Mild Edgar Atheling, a stripling boy,
His brother, heir to England's throne, appears;
The dawn of youth on his fresh cheek; and, lo!
The broadswords glitter as the tartaned troops
March to the pibroch's sound. The Danish trump
Brays like a gong, heard to the holts and towns
Of Lincolnshire.
With crests and shields the same,
A lion frowning on each helmet's cone,
Like the two brothers famed in ancient song,
Godwin and Edmund, sons of Harold, lead
From Scandinavia and the Baltic isles
The impatient Northmen to the embattled host
On Humber's side. The standards wave in air,
Drums roll, and glittering columns file, and arms
Flash to the morn, and bannered-trumpets bray,
Heralds or armourers from tent to tent

Are hurrying; crests, and spears, and steel-bows gleam,
Far as the eye can reach; barbed horses neigh,
Their mailed riders wield the battle-axe,
Or draw the steel-bows with a clang; and, hark!
From the vast moving host is heard one shout,
Conquest or death!—as now the sun ascends,
And on the bastioned walls of Ravenspur
Flings its first beam—one mighty shout is heard,
Perish the Norman! Soldiers, on!—to York!

CANTO FIRST

Castle of Ravenspur, on the Humber—Daughter of Harold—Ailric, the monk

Let us go up to the west turret's top,
Adela cried; let us go up—the night
Is still, and to the east great ocean's hum
Is scarcely heard. If but a wandering step,
Or distant shout, or dip of hastening oar,
Or tramp of steed, or far-off trumpet, break
The hushed horizon, we can catch the sound
When breathless expectation watches there.
Upon the platform of the highest tower
Of Ravenspur, beneath the lonely lamp,
At midnight, leaning o'er the battlement,
The daughter of slain Harold, Adela,
And a gray monk who never left her side,
Watched: for this night or death or victory
The Saxon standard waits.
Hark! 'twas a shout,
And sounds at distance as of marching men!
No! all is silent, save the tide, that rakes,
At times, the beach, or breaks beneath the cliff.
Listen! was it the fall of hastening oars?
No! all is hushed! Oh! when will they return?
Adela sighed; for three long nights had passed,
Since her brave brothers left these bastioned walls,
And marched, with the confederate host, to York.
They come not: Have they perished? So dark thoughts
Arose, and then she raised her look to heaven,
And clasped the cross, and prayed more fervently.
Her lifted eye in the pale lamp-light shone,
Touched with a tear; soft airs of ocean blew
Her long light hair, whilst audibly she cried,
Preserve them, blessed Mary! oh! preserve
My brothers! As she prayed, one pale small star,

A still and lonely star, through the black night
Looked out, like hope! Instant, a trumpet rang,
And voices rose, and hurrying lights appeared;
Now louder shouts along the platform peal—
Oh! they are Normans! she exclaimed, and grasped
The old man's hand, and said, Yet we will die
As Harold's daughter; and, with mien and voice,
Firm and unfaltering, kissed the crucifix.
They knelt together, and the old man spoke:
All here is toil and tempest—we shall go,
Daughter of Harold, where the weary rest.
Oh! holy Mary, 'tis the clank of steel
Up the stone stairs! and, lo! beneath the lamp,
In arms, the beaver of his helmet raised,
Some light hairs straying on his ruddy cheek,
With breath hastily drawn, and cheering smile,
Young Atheling: The Saxon banner waves!
Oh! are my brothers safe? cried Adela,
Speak! speak! oh! tell me, do my brothers live?
Atheling answered: They will soon appear;
My post was on the eastern hills, a scout
Came breathless, sent from Edmund, and I hied,
With a small company, and horses fleet,
At his command, to thee. He bade me say,
Even now, upon the citadel of York,
Above the bursting fires, and rolling smoke,
The Saxon banner waves.
I thank thee, Lord!
My brothers live! cried Adela, and knelt
Upon the platform, with uplifted hands,
And look to heaven;—then rising, with a smile:
We have watched, I and this old man here,
Hour after hour, through the long lingering night,
And now 'tis almost morning: I will stay
Till I have heard my brother's distant horn
From the west woods;—but you are weary, youth?
Oh, no! I will keep watch with you till dawn;
To me most soothing is an hour like this!
And who that saw, as now, the morning stars
Begin to pale, and the gray twilight steal
So calmly on the seas, and wide-hushed world,
Could deem there was a sound of misery
On earth; nay, who could hear thy gentle voice,
Fair maid, and think there was a voice of hate
Or strife beneath the stillness of that cope
Above us! Oh! I hate the noise of arms—
Here will I watch with you. Then, after pause,
Poor England is not what it once has been;

And strange are both our fortunes.
Atheling,
(Adela answered) early piety
Hath disciplined my heart to every change.
How didst thou pass in safety from this land
Of slavery and sorrow?
He replied:
When darker jealousy and lowering hate
Sat on the brow of William, England mourned,
And one dark spirit of conspiracy
Muttered its curses through the land. 'Twas then,
With fiercer glare, the lion's eye was turned
On me:—My sisters and myself embarked—
The wide world was before us—we embarked,
With some few faithful friends, and from the sea
Gazed tearful, for a moment, on the shores
We left for ever (so it then appeared).
Poor Margaret hid her face; but the fresh wind
Swelled the broad mainsail, and the lessening land,
The towers, the spires, the villages, the smoke,
Were seen no more.
When now at sea, the winds
Blew adverse, for to Holland was our course:
More fearful rose the storm; the east wind sang
Louder, till wrecked upon the shores of Forth
Our vessel lay. Here, friendless, we implored
A short sojourn and succour. Scotland's king
Then sat in Dunfermline; he heard the tale
Of our distress, and flew himself to save;
But when he saw my sister Margaret,
Young, innocent, and beautiful in tears,
His heart was moved.
Oh! welcome here, he cried:
'Tis Heaven hath led you. Lady, look on me—
If such a flower be cast to the bleak winds,
'Twere meet I took and wore it next my heart.
Judged he not well, fair maid?
Thou know'st the rest;
Compassion nurtured love, and Margaret
(Such are the events of ruling Providence)
Is now all Scotland's queen!
To join the bands
Of warriors in one cause assembled here,
King Malcolm left his land of hills; his arm
Might make the Conqueror tremble on his throne!
Even should we fail, my sister Margaret
Would love and honour you; and I might hope,
(Oh! might I?) on the banks of Tay or Tweed

With thee to wander, where no curfew sounds,
And mark the summer sun, beyond the hills,
Sink in its glory, and then, hand in hand,
Wind through the woods, and—
Adela replied,
With smile complacent, Listen; I will be
(So to beguile the creeping hours of time)
A tale-teller. Two years we held sojourn
In Denmark; two long weary years, and sighed
When, looking on the southern deep, we thought
Of our poor country. Give me men and ships!
Godwin still cried; oh! give me men and ships!
The king commanded, and his armament—
A mightier never stemmed the Baltic deep,
Sent forth by sea-kings of the north, or bent
On hardier enterprise; for not some isle
Of the lone Orcades was now the prize,
But England's throne.
His mighty armament
Now left the shores of Denmark. Our brave ships
Burst through the Baltic straits, how gloriously!
I heard the trumpets ring; I saw the sails
Of nigh three hundred war-ships, the dim verge
Of the remote horizon's skiey track
Bestudding, here and there, like gems of light
Dropped from the radiance of the morning sun
On the gray waste of waters. So our ships
Swept o'er the billows of the north, and steered
Right on to England.
Foremost of the fleet
Our gallant vessel rode; around the mast
Emblazoned shields were ranged, and plumed crests
Shook as the north-east rose. Upon the prow,
More ardent, Godwin, my brave brother, stood,
And milder Edmund, on whose mailed arm
I hung, when the white waves before us swelled,
And parted. The broad banner, in full length,
Streamed out its folds, on which the Saxon horse
Ramped, as impatient on the land to leap,
To which the winds still bore it bravely on;
Whilst the red cross on the front banner shone,
The hoar deep crimsoning.
Winds, bear us on;
Bear us as cheerily, till white Albion's cliffs
Resound to our triumphant shouts; till there,
On his own Tower, that frowns above the Thames,
Even there we plant these banners and this cross,
And stamp the Conqueror and his crown to dust!

They would have kept me on a foreign shore;
But could I leave my brothers! I with them
Grew up, with them I left my native land,
With them all perils have I braved, of sea
Or war, all storms of hard adversity;
Let death betide, I reck not; all I ask
Is yet once more, in this sad world, to kneel
Upon my father's grave, and kiss the earth.
When the fourth morning gleamed along the deep,
England, Old England! burst the general cry:
England, Old England! Every eye, intent,
Was turned; and Godwin pointed with his sword
To Flamborough, pale rising o'er the surge.
Nearer into the kingdom's heart bear on
The death-storm of our vengeance! Godwin cried.
Soon, like a cloud, the northern Foreland rose—
Know ye those cliffs, towering in giant state!
But, hark! along the shores alarum-bells
Ring out more loud, blast answers blast, the swords
Of hurrying horsemen, and projected spears,
Flash to the sun. On yonder castle walls
A thousand bows are bent; again our course
Back to the north is turned. Now twilight veiled
The sinking sands of Yarmouth, and we heard
A long deep toll from many a village tower
On shore—and, lo! the scattered inland lights,
That sprinkled winding ocean's lowly verge,
At once are lost in darkness. God in heaven,
It is the curfew! Godwin cried, and smote
His forehead. We all heard that sullen sound
For the first time, that night; but the winds blew,
Our ship sailed out of hearing; yet we thought
Of the poor mother, who, on winter nights,
When her belated husband from the wood
Was not come back, her lonely taper lit,
And turned the glass, and saw the faggot-flame
Shine on the faces of her little ones:
Those times will ne'er return.
Darkness descends;
Again the sun is rising o'er the waves;
And now hoarse Humber roars beneath our keels,
And we have landed
Yea, and struck a blow,
Such as may make the crowned Conqueror quail,
Edgar replied.
Grant Heaven that we may live,
Adela cried, in love and peace again,
When every storm is past. But this good man

Is silent. Ailric, does no hope, even now,
Arise on thy dark heart? Good father, speak!
With aspect mild, on which its fitful light
The watch-tower lamp threw pale, the monk replied:
Youth, on thy light hair and ingenuous brow
Most comely sits the morn of life; on me,
And this bare head, the night of time descends
In sorrow. I look back upon the past,
And think of joy and sadness upon earth,
Like the vast ocean's fluctuating toil
From everlasting! I have seen its waste
Now in the sunshine sleeping; now high-ridged
With storms; and such the kingdoms of the earth.
Yes, youth, and flattering fortune, and the light
Of summer days, are as the radiance
That flits along the solitary waves,
Even whilst we gaze, and say, How beautiful!
So fitful and so perishing the dream
Of human things! But there is light above,
Undying; and, at times, faint harmonies
Heard, by the weary pilgrim, in his way
O'er perilous rocks, and through unwatered wastes,
Who looks up, fainting, and prays earnestly
To pass into that rest, whence sounds so sweet
Come, whispering of hope; else it were best
Beneath the load the forlorn heart endures
To sink at once; to shut the eyes on things
That sear the sight; and so to wrap the soul
In sullen, tearless, ruthless apathy.
Therefore, 'midst every human change, I drop
A tear upon the cross, and all is calm;
Yea, full of blissful and of brightest views,
On this dark tide of time.
Youth, thou hast known
Adversity; even in thy morn of life,
The springtide rainbow fades, and many days,
And many years, perchance, of weal or woe
Hang o'er thee! happy, if through every change
Thy constant heart, thy steadfast view, be fixed
Upon that better kingdom, where the crown
Immortal is held out to holy hope,
Beyond the clouds that rest upon the grave.
Oh! I remember when King Harold stood
Blooming in youth like thee; I saw him crowned—
I heard the loud voice of a nation hail
His rising star; then, flaming in mid-heaven
The red portentous comet, like the hand
Upon the wall, came forth: its fatal course

All marked, and gazed in terror, as it looked
With lurid light upon this land. It passed;
Old men had many bodings; but I saw,
Reckless, King Harold, in his plumed helm,
Ride foremost of the mailed chivalry,
That, when the fierce Norwegian passed the seas,
Met his host man to man; I saw the sword,
Advanced and glittering, in the victor's hand,
That smote the Hardrada to the earth! To-day
King Harold rose, like an avenging God;
To-morrow (so it seemed, so short the space),
To-morrow, through the field of blood, we sought
His mangled corse amid the heaps of slain:
Shall I recount the event more faithfully?
Its spectred memory never since that hour
Has left my heart.
William was in his tent,
Spread on the battle-plain, on that same night
When seventy thousand dead lay at his feet;
They who, at sunrise, with bent bows and spears,
Confronted and defied him, at his feet
Lay dead! Alone he watches in his tent,
At midnight; 'midst a sight so terrible
We came; we stood before him, where he sat,
I and my brother Osgood. Who are ye?
Sternly he asked; and Osgood thus replied:
Conqueror, and lord, and soon to be a king,
We, two poor monks of Waltham Abbey, kneel
Before thee, sorrowing! He who is slain
To us was bountiful. He raised those walls
Where we devote our life to prayer and praise.
Oh! by the mercies which the God of all
Hath shewn to thee this day, grant our request;
To search for his dead body, through this field
Of terror, that his bones may rest with us.
Your king hath met the meed of broken faith,
William replied. But yet he shall not want
A sepulchre; and on this very spot
My purpose stands, as I have vowed to God,
To build a holy monastery: here,
A hundred monks shall pray for all who fell
In this dread strife; and your King Harold here
Shall have due honours and a stately tomb.
Still on our knees, we answered, Oh! not so,
Dread sovereign;—hear us, of your clemency.
We beg his body; beg it for the sake
Of our successors; beg it for ourselves,
That we may bury it in the same spot

Himself ordained when living; where the choirs
May sing for his repose, in distant years,
When we are dust and ashes.
Then go forth,
And search for him, at the first dawn of day,
King William said. We crossed our breasts, and passed,
Slow rising, from his presence. So we went,
In silence, to the quarry of the dead.
The sun rose on that still and dismal host;
Toiling from corse to corse, we trod in blood,
From morn till noon toiling, and then I said,
Seek Editha, her whom he loved. She came;
And through the field of death she passed: she looked
On many a face, ghastly upturned; her hand
Unloosed the helmet, smoothed the clotted hair,
And many livid hands she took in hers;
Till, stooping o'er a mangled corse, she shrieked,
Then into tears burst audibly, and turned
Her face, and with a faltering voice pronounced,
Oh, Harold! We took up, and bore the corse
From that sad spot, and washed the ghastly wound
Deep in the forehead, where the broken barb
Was fixed.
So weltering from the field, we bore
King Harold's corse. A hundred Norman knights
Met the sad train, with pikes that trailed the ground.
Our old men prayed, and spoke of evil days
To come; the women smote their breasts and wept;
The little children knelt beside the way,
As on to Waltham the funereal car
Moved slow. Few and disconsolate the train
Of English earls, for few, alas! remained;
So many in the field of death lay cold.
The horses slowly paced, till Waltham towers
Before us rose. There, with long tapered blaze,
Our brethren met us, chanting, two and two,
The "Miserere" of the dead. And there—
But, my child Adela, you are in tears—
There at the foot of the high altar lies
The last of Saxon kings. Sad Editha,
At distance, watched the rites, and from that hour
We never saw her more.
A distant trump
Now rung—again!—again!—and thrice a trump
Has answered from the walls of Ravenspur.
My brothers! they are here! Adela cried,
And left the tower in breathless ardour. York
Flames to the sky! a general voice was heard—

The drawbridge clanks; into the inner court
A mailed man rides on—York is no more!
The cry without redoubles. On the ground
The rider flung his bloody sword, and raised
His helm, dismounting: the first dawn of day
Gleamed on the shattered plume. Oh! Adela,
He cried, your brother Godwin! and she flew,
And murmuring, My brave brother! hid her face,
Clasping his mailed breast. Soon gazing round,
She cried, But where is Edmund? Was he wont
To linger?
Edmund has a sacred charge,
Godwin replied. But trust his anxious love,
We soon shall hear his voice. I need some rest—
'Tis now broad day; but we have watched and fought:
I can sleep sound, though the shrill bird of morn
Mount and upbraid my slumbers with her song.
Tranquil and clear the autumnal day declined:
The barks at anchor cast their lengthened shades
On the gray bastioned walls; airs from the deep
Wandered, and touched the cordage as they passed,
Then hovered with expiring breath, and stirred
Scarce the quiescent pennant; the bright sea
Lay silent in its glorious amplitude,
Without; far up, in the pale atmosphere,
A white cloud, here and there, hung overhead,
And some red freckles streaked the horizon's edge,
Far as the sight could reach; beneath the rocks,
That reared their dark brows beetling o'er the bay,
The gulls and guillemots, with short quaint cry,
Just broke the sleeping stillness of the air,
Or, skimming, almost touched the level main,
With wings far seen, and more intensely white,
Opposed to the blue space; whilst Panope
Played in the offing. Humber's ocean-stream,
Inland, went sounding on, by rocks and sands
And castle, yet so sounding as it seemed
A voice amidst the hushed and listening world
That spoke of peace; whilst from the bastion's point
One piping red-breast might almost be heard.
Such quiet all things hushed, so peaceable
The hour: the very swallows, ere they leave
The coast to pass a long and weary way
O'er ocean's solitude, seem to renew
Once more their summer feelings, as a light
So sweet would last for ever, whilst they flock
In the brief sunshine of the turret-top.
'Twas at this hour of evening, Adela

And Godwin, now restored by rest, went forth,
Linked arm in arm, upon the eastern beach,
Beyond the headland's shade. If such an hour
Seemed smiling on the heart, how smiled it now
To him who yesternight, a soldier, stood
Amid the direst sight of human strife
And bloodshed; heard the cries, the trumpet's blast,
Ring o'er the dying; saw, with all its towers,
A city blazing to the midnight sky,
And mangled groups of miserable men,
Gasping or dead, whilst with his iron heel
He splashed the blood beneath! How changed the scene!
The sun's last light upon the battlements,
The sea, the landscape, the peace-breathing air,
Remembered both of the departed hours
Of early life, when once they had a home,
A country, where their father wore a crown.
What changes since that time, for them and all
They loved! how many found an early grave,
Cut off by the red sword! how many mourned,
Scattered by various fates, through distant lands!
How desolate their own poor country, bound
By the oppressor's chain! As thoughts like these
Arose, the bells of rural Nevilthorpe
Rang out a joyous peal, rang merrily,
For tidings heard from York: their melody
Mingled with things forgotten. Until then,
And then remembered freshly, Adela
That instant turned to hide her tears, and saw
Her brother Edmund leading by the hand
A boy of lovely mien and footstep light
Along the sands. My sister, Edmund cried,
See here a footpage I have brought from York
To serve a lady fair! The boy held out
His hand to Adela, as he would say,
Look, and protect me, lady. Adela,
Advancing with a smile and glowing cheek,
Cried, Welcome, truant brother; and then took
The child's right hand, and said, My pretty page,
And have you not a tale to tell to me?
The boy spake nothing, but looked earnestly
And anxiously at Edmund. Edmund said,
If he is silent, I must speak for him.
'Twas when the minster flamed, and, sword in hand,
Godwin, and Waltheof, and stern Hereward,
Directed the red slaughter; black with smoke
I burst into the citadel, and saw,
Not the grim warder, with his huge axe up,

But o'er her child, a frantic mother, mute
With horror, in delirious agony,
Clasping it to her bosom; stern and still
The father stood, his hand upon his brow,
As praying, in that hour, that God might make,
In mercy, the last trial brief. Fear not—
I am a man—nay, fear not me, I cried,
And seizing this child's hand, in safety placed,
Amidst the smoke, and sounds and sights of death,
Him and his mother! She with bursting heart
Knelt down to bless me: when I saw that boy,
So beautiful, I thought of Adela,
And said, Oh! trust with his preserver him
Whom every eye must view with tender love,
Oh! trust me; for his safety, lo! I pledge
My honour and my life.
And I have brought
My trusted charge, that you, my Adela,
May show him gentler courtesy than those
Whom war in its stern trade has almost steeled.
His sister kissed the child's light hair and cheek,
And folded his small hands in hers, and said,
You shall be my true knight, and wear a plume,
Wilt thou not, boy; and for a lady's love
Fight, like a valiant soldier! I will die,
The poor child said, for friends like those who saved
My father and my mother; and again
Adela kissed his forehead and his eyes,
And said, But we are Saxons!
As she spoke,
The winds began to muster, and the sea
Swelled with a sound more solemn, whilst the sun
Was sinking, and its last and lurid light
Streaked the long line of cumbrous clouds, that hung
In wild red masses o'er the murmuring deep,
Now flickering fast with foam. The sea-fowl flew
Rapidly on, o'er the black-lifted surge,
Borne down the wind, and then was seen no more.
Meantime the dark deep wilder heaves, and, hark!
Heavily overhead the gathered storm
Comes sounding!
Haste!—and in the castle-keep
List to the winds and waves that roar without.

CANTO SECOND

Waltham Forest—Tower—William and his Barons

There had been fearful sounds in the air last night
In the wild wolds of Holderness, when York
Flamed to the midnight sky, and spells of death
Were heard amidst the depth of Waltham woods;
For there the wan and weird sisters met
Their imps, and the dark spirits that rejoice
When foulest deeds are done on earth, and there
In dread accordance rose their dismal joy.

SPIRITS AND NIGHT-HAGS
Around, around, around,
Troop and dance we to the sound,
Whilst mocking imps cry, Ho! ho! ho!
On earth there will be woe! more woe!

SPIRIT OF THE EARTHQUAKE
Arise, swart fiends, 'tis I command;
Burst your caves, and rock the land.

SPIRIT OF THE STORM
Loud tempests, sweep the conscious wood!

SPIRIT OF THE BATTLE
I scent from earth more blood! more blood!

SPIRIT OF THE FIRE
When the wounded cry,
And the craven die,
I will ride on the spires,
And the red volumes of the bursting fires.

SPIRITS AND NIGHT-HAGS
Around, around, around,
Dance we to the dismal sound
Of dying cries and mortal woe,
Whilst mocking imps shout, Ho! ho! ho!

FIRST SPIRIT
Hear!
Spirits that our 'hests perform
In the earthquake or the storm,
Appear, appear!

A fire is lighted—the pale smoke goes up;
Obscure, terrific features through the clouds
Are seen, and a wild laughter heard, We come!

FIRST MINISTERING SPIRIT
I have syllables of dread;
They can wake the dreamless dead.

SECOND SPIRIT
I, a dark sepulchral song,
That can lead hell's phantom-throng.

THIRD SPIRIT
Like a nightmare I will rest
This night upon King William's breast!

SPIRITS AND NIGHT-HAGS
Around, around, around,
Dance we to the dismal sound
Of dying shrieks and mortal woe,
Whilst antic imps shout, Ho! ho! ho!

They vanished, and the earth shook where they stood.

That night, King William first within the Tower
Received his vassal barons; in that Tower
Which oft since then has echoed to night-shrieks
Of secret murder, or the lone lament.
Now other sounds were heard, for on this night
Its canopied and vaulted chambers rang
With minstrelsy; whilst sounds of long acclaim
Re-echoed, from the loopholes, o'er the Thames
The drawbridge, and the ponderous cullis-gate,
Frowned on the moat; the flanking towers aspired
O'er the embattled walls, where proudly waved
The Norman banner. William, laugh to scorn
The murmurs of conspiracy and hate
That round thee gather, like the storms of night
Mustering, when murder hides her visored mien!
Now, what hast thou to fear! Let the fierce Dane
Into the centre of thy kingdom sweep,
With hostile armament, even like the tide
Of the hoarse Humber, on whose waves he rode!
Let foes confederate; let one voice of hate,
One cry of instant vengeance, one deep curse
Be heard, from Waltham woods to Holderness!
Let Waltheof, stern in steel; let Hereward,
Impatient as undaunted, flash their swords;
Let the boy Edgar, backed by Scotland's king,
Advance his feeble claim, and don his casque,

Whose brows might better a blue bonnet grace;
Let Edwin and vindictive Morcar join
The sons of Harold,—what hast thou to fear?
London's sole Tower might laugh their strength to scorn!
Upon that night when York's proud castle fell,
Here William held his court. The torches glared
On crest and crozier. Knights and prelates bowed
Before their sovereign. He, his knights and peers
Surveying with a stern complacency,
Inclined not from his seat, o'ercanopied
With golden valance, woven by no hand,
Save of the Queen. Yet calm his countenance
Shone, and his brow a dignified repose
Marked kingly; high his forehead, and besprent
With dark hair, interspersed with gray; his eye
Glanced amiable, chiefly when the light
Of a brief smile attempered majesty.
His beard was dark and heavy, yet diffused,
Low as the lion ramping on his breast
Engrailed upon the mail.
Odo approached,
And knelt, then rising, placed the diadem
Upon his brow, with laurels intertwined.
Again the voice of acclamation rang,
And from the galleries a hundred harps
Resounded Roland's song! Long live the King!
The barons, and the prelates, and the knights,
Long live the Conqueror! cried; a god on earth!
That instant the high vaulted chamber shook
As with a blast from heaven, and all was mute
Around him, and the very fortress rocked,
As it would topple on their heads. He rose
Disturbed and frowning, for tumultuous thoughts
Crowded like night upon his heart; then waved
His hand. The barons, abbots, knights retire.
Behold him now alone! before a lamp
A crucifix appears; upon the ground
Lies the same sword that Hastings' battle dyed
Deep to the hilt in gore; behold, he kneels
And prays, Thou only, Lord, art ever great;
Have mercy on my sins! The crucifix
Shook as he spoke, shook visibly, and, hark!
There is a low moan, as of dying men,
At distance heard.
Then William first knew fear.
He had heard tumults of the battle-field,
The noise, the glorious hurrahs, and the clang
Of trumpets round him, but no sound like this

Ere smote with unknown terror on his heart,
As if the eye of God that moment turned
And saw it beating.
Rising slow, he flung
Upon a couch his agitated limbs;
The lamp was near him; on the ground his sword
And helmet lay; short troubled slumbers stole,
And darkly rose the spirit of his dream.
He saw a field of blood,—it passed away;
A glittering palace rose, with mailed men
Thronged, and the voice of multitudes was heard
Acclaiming: suddenly the sounds had ceased,
The glittering palace vanished, and, behold!
Long winding cloisters, echoing to the chant
Of stoled fathers; and the mass-song ceased—
Then a dark tomb appeared, and, lo! a shape
As of a phantom-king!
Nearer it came,
And nearer yet, in silence, through the gloom.
Advancing—still advancing: the cold glare
Of armour shone as it approached, and now
It stands o'er William's couch! The spectre gazed
A while, then lifting its dark visor up—
Horrible vision!—shewed a grisly wound
Deep in its forehead, and therein appeared
Gouts, as yet dropping from an arrow's point
Infixed! And that red arrow's deadly barb
The shadow drew, and pointed at the breast
Of William; and the blood dropped on his breast;
And through his steely arms one drop of blood
Came cold as death's own hand upon his heart!
Whilst a deep voice was heard, Now sleep in peace,
I am avenged!
Starting, he exclaimed,
Hence, horrid phantom! Ho! Fitzalain, ho!
Montgomerie! Each baron, with a torch,
Before him stood. By dawn of day, he cried,
We will to horse. What passes in our thoughts
We shall unfold hereafter. By St Anne,
Albeit, not ten thousand phantoms sent
By the dead Harold can divert our course,
They may bear timely warning.
'Tis yet night—
Give me a battle-song ere daylight dawns;
The song of Roland, or of Charlemagne—
Or our own fight at Hastings.
Torches! ho!
And let the gallery blaze with lights! Awake,

Harpers of Normandy, awake! By Heaven,
I will not sleep till your full chords ring out
The song of England's conquest! Torches! ho!
He spoke. Again the blazing gallery
Echoed the harpers' song. Old Eustace led
The choir, and whilst the king paced to and fro,
Thus rose the bold, exulting symphony.

SONG OF THE BATTLE OF HASTINGS

The Norman armament beneath thy rocks, St Valerie,
Is moored; and, streaming to the morn, three hundred banners fly,
Of crimson silk; with golden cross, effulgent o'er the rest,
That banner, proudest in the fleet, streams, which the Lord had blessed.
The gale is fair, the sails are set, cheerily the south wind blows,
And Norman archers, all in steel, have grasped their good yew-bows;
Aloud the harpers strike their harps, whilst morning light is flung
Upon the cross-bows and the shields, that round the masts are hung.
Speed on, ye brave! 'tis William leads; bold barons, at his word,
Lo! sixty thousand men of might for William draw the sword.

So, bound to England's southern shore, we rolled upon the seas,
And gallantly the white sails set were, and swelling to the breeze.
On, on, to victory or death! now rose the general cry;
The minstrels sang, On, on, ye brave, to death or victory!
Mark yonder ship, how straight she steers; ye knights and barons brave,
'Tis William's ship, and proud she rides, the foremost o'er the wave.
And now we hailed the English coast, and, lo! on Beachy Head,
The radiance of the setting sun majestical is shed.
The fleet sailed on, till, Pevensey! we saw thy welcome strand;
Duke William now his anchor casts, and dauntless leaps to land.

The English host, by Harold led, at length appear in sight,
And now they raise a deafening shout, and stand prepared for fight;
The hostile legions halt a while, and their long lines display,
Now front to front they stand, in still and terrible array.
Give out the word, God, and our right! rush like a storm along,
Lift up God's banner, and advance, resounding Roland's song!
Ye spearmen, poise your lances well, by brave Montgomerie led,
Ye archers, bend your bows, and draw your arrows to the head.
They draw—the bent bows ring—huzzah! another flight, and hark!
How the sharp arrowy shower beneath the sun goes hissing dark.

Hark! louder grows the deadly strife, till all the battle-plain
Is red with blood, and heaped around with men and horses slain.
On, Normans, on! Duke William cried, and Harold, tremble thou,

Now think upon thy perjury, and of thy broken vow.
The banner of thy armed knight, thy shield, thy helm are vain—
The fatal shaft has sped,—by Heaven! it hisses in his brain!
So William won the English crown, and all his foemen beat,
And Harold, and his Britons brave, lay silent at his feet.
Enough! the day is breaking, cried the King:
Away! away! be armed at my side,
Without attendants, and to horse, to horse!

CANTO THIRD

Waltham Abbey and Forest—Wild Woman of the Woods

At Waltham Abbey, o'er King Harold's grave
A requiem was chanted; for last night
A passing spirit shook the battlements,
And the pale monk, at midnight, as he watched
The lamp, beheld it tremble; whilst the shrines
Shook, as the deep foundations of the fane
Were moved. Oh! pray for Harold's soul! he cried.
And now, at matin bell, the monks were met,
And slowly pacing round the grave, they sang:

DIRGE
Peace, oh! peace, be to the shade
Of him who here in earth is laid:
Saints and spirits of the blessed,
Look upon his bed of rest;
Forgive his sins, propitious be;
Dona pacem, Domine,
Dona pacem, Domine!

When, from yonder window's height,
The moonbeams on the floor are bright,
Sounds of viewless harps shall die,
Sounds of heaven's own harmony!
Forgive his sins, propitious be;
Dona pacem, Domine,
Dona pacem, Domine!

By the spirits of the brave,
Who died the land they loved to save;
By the soldier's faint farewell,
By freedom's blessing, where he fell;
Forgive his sins, propitious be;
Dona pacem, Domine,
Dona pacem, Domine!

By a nation's mingled moan,
By liberty's expiring groan,
By the saints, to whom 'tis given
To bear that parting groan to heaven;
To his shade propitious be;
Dona pacem, Domine,
Dona pacem, Domine!

The proud and mighty—

As they sung, the doors
Of the west portal, with a sound that shook
The vaulted roofs, burst open; and, behold!
An armed Norman knight, the helmet closed
Upon his visage, but of stature tall,
His coal-black armour clanking as he trod,
Advancing up the middle aisle alone,
Approached: he gazed in silence on the grave
Of the last Saxon; there a while he stood,
Then knelt a moment, muttering a brief prayer:
The fathers crossed their breasts—the mass-song ceased;
Heedless of all around, the mailed man
Rose up, nor speaking, nor inclining, paced
Back through the sounding aisle, and left the fane.
The monks their interrupted song renewed:

The proud and mighty, when they die,
With the crawling worm shall lie;
But who would not a crown resign,
Harold, for a rest like thine!
Saviour Lord, propitious be;
Dona pacem, Domine,
Dona pacem, Domine!

"Pacem" (as slow the stoled train retire),
"Pacem," the shrines and fretted roofs returned.
'Twas told, three Norman knights, in armour, spurred
Their foaming steeds to the West Abbey door;
But who it was, that with his visor closed
Passed up the long and echoing fane alone,
And knelt on Harold's gravestone, none could tell.
The stranger knights in silence left the fane,
And soon were lost in the surrounding shades
Of Waltham forest.
He who foremost rode
Passed his companions, on his fleeter steed,
And, muttering in a dark and dreamy mood,

Spurred on alone, till, looking round, he heard
Only the murmur of the woods above,
Whilst soon all traces of a road were lost
In the inextricable maze. From morn
Till eve, in the wild woods he wandered lost.
Night followed, and the gathering storm was heard
Among the branches. List! there is no sound
Of horn far off, or tramp of toiling steed,
Or call of some belated forester;
No lonely taper lights the waste; the woods
Wave high their melancholy boughs, and bend
Beneath the rising tempest. Heard ye not
Low thunder to the north! The solemn roll
Redoubles through the darkening forest deep,
That sounds through all its solitude, and rocks,
As the long peal at distance rolls away.
Hark! the loud thunder crashes overhead;
And, as the red fire flings a fitful glare,
The branches of old oaks, and mossy trunks,
Distinct and visible shine out; and, lo!
Interminable woods, a moment seen,
Then lost again in deeper, lonelier night.
The torrent rain o'er the vast leafy cope
Comes sounding, and the drops fall heavily
Where the strange knight is sheltered by the trunk
Of a huge oak, whose dripping branches sweep
Far round. Oh! happy, if beneath the flash
Some castle's bannered battlements were seen,
Where the lone minstrel, as the storm of night
Blew loud without, beside the blazing hearth
Might dry his hoary locks, and strike his harp
(The fire relumined in his aged eyes)
To songs of Charlemagne!
Or, happier yet
If some gray convent's bell remote proclaimed
The hour of midnight service, when the chant
Was up, and the long range of windows shone
Far off on the lone woods; whilst Charity
Might bless and welcome, in a night like this,
The veriest outcast! Angel of the storm,
Ha! thy red bolt this instant shivering rives
That blasted oak!
The horse starts back, and bounds
From the knight's grasp. The way is dark and wild;
As dark and wild as if the solitude
Had never heard the sound of human steps.
Pondering he stood, when, by the lightning's glance,
The knight now marked a small and craggy path

Descending through the woody labyrinth.
He tracked his way slowly from brake to brake,
Till now he gained a deep sequestered glen.
I fear not storms, nor thunders, nor the sword,
The knight exclaimed: that eye alone I fear,
God's stern and steadfast eye upon the heart!
Yet peace is in the grave where Harold sleeps.
Who speaks of Harold? cried a woman's voice,
Heard through the deep night of the woods. He spoke,
A stern voice answered, he of Harold spoke,
Who feared his sword in the red front of war,
Less than the powers of darkness: and he crossed
His breast, for at that instant rose the thought
Of the weird sisters of the wold, that mock
Night wanderers, and "syllable men's names"
In savage solitude. If now, he cried,
Dark minizar, thy spells of wizard power
Have raised the storm and wild winds up, appear!
He scarce had spoken, when, by the red flash
That glanced along the glen, half visible,
Uprose a tall, majestic female form:
So visible, her eyes' intenser light
Shone wildly through the darkness; and her face,
On which one pale flash more intently shone,
Was like a ghost's by moonlight, as she stood
A moment seen: her lips appeared to move,
Muttering, whilst her long locks of ebon hair
Streamed o'er her forehead, by the bleak winds blown
Upon her heaving breast.
The knight advanced;
The expiring embers from a cave within,
Now wakened by the night-air, shot a light,
Fitful and trembling, and this human form,
If it were human, at the entrance stood,
As seemed, of a rude cave. You might have thought
She had strange spells, such a mysterious power
Was round her; such terrific solitude,
Such night, as of the kingdom of the grave;
Whilst hurricanes seemed to obey her 'hest.
And she no less admired, when, front to front,
By the rekindling ember's darted gleam,
A mailed man, of proud illustrious port,
She marked; and thus, but with unfaltering voice,
She spake:
Yes! it was Harold's name I heard!
Whence, and what art thou? I have watched the night,
And listened to the tempest as it howled;
And whilst I listening lay, methought I heard,

Even now, the tramp as of a rushing steed;
Therefore I rose, and looked into the dark,
And now I hear one speak of Harold: say,
Whence, and what art thou, solitary man?
If lost and weary, enter this poor shed;
If wretched, pray with me; if on dark deeds
Intent, I am a most poor woman, cast
Into the depths of mortal misery!
The desolate have nought to lose:—pass on!
I had not spoken, but for Harold's name,
By thee pronounced: it sounded in my ears
As of a better world—ah, no! of days
Of happiness in this. Whence, who art thou?
I am a Norman, woman; more to know
Seek not:—and I have been to Harold's grave,
Remembering that the mightiest are but dust;
And I have prayed the peace of God might rest
Upon his soul.
And, by our blessed Lord,
The deed was holy, that lone woman said;
And may the benediction of all saints,
Whoe'er thou art, rest on thy head. But say,
What perilous mischance hath hither led
Thy footsteps in an hour and night like this?
Over his grave, of whom we spake, I heard
The mass-song sung. I knelt upon that grave,
And prayed for my own sins, I left the fane,
And heard the chanted rite at distance die.
Returning through these forest shades, with thoughts
Not of this world, I pressed my panting steed,
The foremost of the Norman knights, and passed
The track, that, leading to the forest-ford,
Winds through the opening thickets; on a height
I stood and listened, but no voice replied:
The storm descended; at the lightning's flash
My good steed burst the reins, and frantic fled.
I was alone: the small and craggy path
Led to this solitary glen; and here,
As dark and troubled thoughts arose, I mused
Upon the dead man's sleep; for God, I thought,
This night spoke in the rocking of the winds!
There is a Judge in heaven, the woman said,
Who seeth all things; and there is a voice,
Inaudible 'midst the tumultuous world,
That speaks of fear or comfort to the heart
When all is still! But shroud thee in this cave
Till morning: such a sojourn may not please
A courtly knight, like echoing halls of joy.

I have but some wild roots, a bed of fern,
And no companion save this bloodhound here,
Who, at my beck, would tear thee to the earth;
Yet enter—fear not! And that poor abode
The proud knight entered, with rain-drenched plume.
Yet here I dwell in peace, the woman said,
Remote from towns, nor start at the dire sound
Of that accursed curfew! Soldier-knight,
Thou art a Norman! Had the invader spurned
All charities in thy own native land,
Yes, thou wouldst know what injured Britons feel!
Nay, Englishwoman, thou dost wrong our king,
The knight replied: conspiracy and fraud
Hourly surrounding him, at last compelled
Stern rigour to awake. What! shall the bird
Of thunder slumber on the citadel,
And blench his eye of fire, when, looking down,
He sees, in ceaseless enmity combined,
Those who would pluck his feathers from his breast,
And cast them to the winds! Woman, on thee,
Haply, the tempest of the times has beat
Too roughly; but thy griefs he can requite.
The indignant woman answered, He requite!
Can he bring back the dead? Can he restore
Joy to the broken-hearted? He requite!
Can he pour plenty on the vales his frown
Has blasted, bid sweet evening hear again
The village pipe, and the fair flowers revive
His bloody footstep crushed? For poverty,
I reck it not: what is to me the night,
Spent cheerless, and in gloom and solitude?
I fix my eye upon that crucifix,
I mourn for those that are not—for my brave,
My buried countrymen! Of this no more!
Thou art a foe; but a brave soldier-knight
Would scorn to wrong a woman; and if death
Could arm my hand this moment, thou wert safe
In a poor cottage as in royal halls.
Here rest a while till morning dawns—the way
No mortal could retrace:—'twill not be long,
And I can cheat the time with some old strain;
For, Norman though thou art, thy soul has felt
Even as a man, when sacred sympathy
This morning led thee to King Harold's grave.
The woman sat beside the hearth, and stirred
The embers, or with fern or brushwood raised
A fitful flame, but cautious, lest its light
Some roving forester might mark. At times,

The small and trembling blaze shone on her face,
Still beautiful, and showed the dark eye's fire
Beneath her long black locks. When she stood up,
A dignity, though in the garb of want,
Seemed round her, chiefly when the brushwood-blaze
Glanced through the gloom, and touched the dusky mail
Of the strange knight; then with sad smile she sung:

Oh! when 'tis summer weather,
And the yellow bee, with fairy sound,
The waters clear is humming round,
And the cuckoo sings unseen,
And the leaves are waving green—
Oh! then 'tis sweet,
In some remote retreat,
To hear the murmuring dove,
With those whom on earth alone we love,
And to wind through the greenwood together.
But when 'tis winter weather,
And crosses grieve,
And friends deceive,
And rain and sleet
The lattice beat,—
Oh! then 'tis sweet
To sit and sing
Of the friends with whom, in the days of spring,
We roamed through the greenwood together.

The bloodhound slept upon the hearth; he raised
His head, and, through the dusk, his eyes were seen,
Fiery, a moment; but again he slept,
When she her song renewed.

Though thy words might well deceive me—
That is past—subdued I bend;
Yet, for mercy, do not leave me
To the world without a friend!
Oh! thou art gone! and would, with thee,
Remembrance too had fled!
She lives to bid me weep, and see
The wreath I cherished dead.

The knight, through the dim lattice, watched the clouds
Of morn, now slowly struggling in the east,
When, with a voice more thrilling, and an air
Wilder, again a sad song she intoned:

Upon the field of blood,

Amidst the bleeding brave,
O'er his pale corse I stood—
But he is in his grave!
I wiped his gory brow,
I smoothed his clotted hair—
But he is at peace, in the cold ground now;
Oh! when shall we meet there?

At once, horns, trumpets, and the shouts of men,
Were heard above the valley. At the sound,
The knight, upstarting from his dreamy trance,
High raised his vizor, and his bugle rang,
Answering. By God in heaven, thou art the king!
The woman said. Again the clarions rung:
Like lightning, Alain and Montgomerie
Spurred through the wood, and led a harnessed steed
To the lone cabin's entrance, whilst the train
Sent up a deafening shout, Long live the king!
He, ere he vaulted to the saddle-bow,
Turned with a look benevolent, and cried,
Barons and lords, to this poor woman here
Haply I owe my life! Let her not need!
Away! she cried, king of these realms, away!
I ask not wealth nor pity—least from thee,
Of all men. As the day began to dawn,
More fixed and dreadful seemed her steadfast look;
The long black hair upon her labouring breast
Streamed, whilst her neck, as in disdain, she raised,
Swelling, her eyes a wild terrific light
Shot, and her voice, with intonation deep,
Uttered a curse, that even the bloodhound crouched
Beneath her feet, whilst with stern look she spoke:
Yes! I am Editha! she whom he loved—
She whom thy sword has left in solitude,
How desolate! Yes, I am Editha!
And thou hast been to Harold's grave—oh! think,
King, where thy own will be! He rests in peace;
But even a spot is to thy bones denied;
I see thy carcase trodden under foot;
Thy children—his, with filial reverence,
Still think upon the spot where he is laid,
Though distant and far severed—but thy son,
Thy eldest born, ah! see, he lifts the sword
Against his father's breast! Hark, hark! the chase
Is up! in that wild forest thou hast made!
The deer is flying—the loud horn resounds—
Hurrah! the arrow that laid Harold low,
It flies, it trembles in the Red King's heart!

Norman, Heaven's hand is on thee, and the curse
Of this devoted land! Hence, to thy throne!
The king a moment with compassion gazed,
And now the clarions, and the horns, and trumps
Rang louder; the bright banners in the winds
Waved beautiful; the neighing steeds aloft
Mantled their manes, and up the valley flew,
And soon have left behind the glen, the cave
Of solitary Editha, and sounds
Of her last agony!
Montgomerie,
King William, turning, cried, when this whole land
Is portioned (for till then we may not hope
For lasting peace) forget not Editha.
In the gray beam the spires of London shone,
And the proud banner on the bastion
Of William's tower was seen above the Thames,
As the gay train, slow winding through the woods,
Approached; when, lo! with spurs of blood, and voice
Faltering, upon a steed, whose labouring chest
Heaved, and whose bit was wet with blood and froth,
A courier met them.
York, O king! he cried,
York is in ashes!—all thy Normans slain!
Now, by the splendour of the throne of God,
King William cried, nor woman, man, nor child,
Shall live! Terrific flashed his eye of fire,
And darker grew his frown; then, looking up,
He drew his sword, and with a vow to Heaven,
Amid his barons, to the trumpet's clang
Rode onward (breathing vengeance) to the Tower.

CANTO FOURTH

Wilds of Holderness—Hags—Parting on the Humber—Waltham Abbey, and Grave—Conclusion

The moon was high, when, 'mid the wildest wolds
Of Holderness, where erst that structure vast,
An idol-temple, in old heathen times,
Frowned with gigantic shadow to the moon,
That oft had heard the dark song and the groans
Of sacrifice,
There the wan sisters met;
They circled the rude stone, and called the dead,
And sung by turns their more terrific song:

FIRST HAG

I looked in the seer's prophetic glass,
And saw the deeds that should come to pass;
From Carlisle-Wall to Flamborough Head,
The reeking soil was heaped with dead.

SECOND HAG

The towns were stirring at dawn of day,
And the children went out in the morn to play;
The lark was singing on holt and hill;
I looked again, but the towns were still;
The murdered child on the ground was thrown,
And the lark was singing to heaven alone.

THIRD HAG

I saw a famished mother lie,
Her lips were livid, and glazed her eye;
The tempest was rising, and sang in the south,
And I snatched the blade of grass from her mouth.

FOURTH HAG

By the rolling of the drums,
Hitherward King William comes!
The night is struggling with the day—
Hags of darkness, hence! away!

William is in the north; the avenging sword
Descended like a whirlwind where he passed;
Slaughter and Famine at his bidding wait,
Like lank, impatient bloodhounds, till he cries,
Pursue! Again the Norman banner floats
Triumphant on the citadel of York,
Where, circled with the blazonry of arms,
Amid his barons, William holds his state.
The boy preserved from death, young Malet, kneels,
With folded hands; his father, mother kneel,
Imploring clemency for Harold's sons;
For Edmund most. Bareheaded Waltheof bends,
And yields the keys! A breathless courier comes:
What tidings? O'er the seas the Danes are fled;
Morcar and Edwin in Northumberland,
Amidst its wildest mountains, seek to hide
Their broken hopes—their troops are all dispersed.
Malcolm alone, and the boy Atheling,
And the two sons of the dead Harold, wait
The winds to bear them to the North away.
Bid forth a thousand spearmen, William cried:
Now, by the resurrection, and the throne

Of God, King Malcolm shall repent the hour
He ere drew sword in England! Hence! away!
The west wind blows, the boat is on the beach,
The clansmen all embarked, the pipe is heard,
Whilst thoughtful Malcolm and young Atheling
Linger the last upon the shore; and there
Are Harold's children, the gray-headed monk,
Godwin, and Edmund, and poor Adela.
Then Malcolm spoke: The lot is cast! oh, fly
From this devoted land, and live with us,
Amidst our lakes and mountains! Adela,
Atheling whispered, does thy heart say Yes?
For in this world we ne'er may meet again.
The brief hour calls—come, Adela, exclaimed
Malcolm, and kindly took her hand. She looked
To heaven, and fell upon her knees, then rose,
And answered:
Sire, when my brave father fell,
We three were exiles on a distant shore;
And never, or in solitude or courts,
Was God forgotten—all is in his hand.
When those whom I had loved from infancy
Here joined the din of arms, I came with them;
With them I have partaken good and ill,
Have in the self-same mother's lap been laid,
The same eye gazed on us with tenderness,
And the same mother prayed prosperity
Might still be ours through life! Alas! our lot
How different!
Yet let them go with you,
I argue not—the first time in our lives,
If it be so, we here shall separate;
Whatever fate betide, I will not go
Till I have knelt upon my father's grave!
'Tis perilous to think, Atheling cried,
Most perilous—how 'scape the Norman's eye?
She turned, and with a solemn calmness said:
If we should perish, at the hour of death
My father will look down from heaven, and say,
Come, my poor child! oh, come where I am blessed!
My brothers, seek your safety. Here I stand
Resolved; and never will I leave these shores
Till I have knelt upon my father's grave!
We never will forsake thee! Godwin cried.
Let death betide, said Edmund, we will go,
Yes! go with thee, or perish!
As he spoke,
The pilot gave the signal. Then farewell!

King Malcolm cried, friends lately met, and now
To part for ever! and he kissed the cheek
Of Adela, and took brave Godwin's hand
And Edmund's, and then said, almost in tears,
It is not now too late! yet o'er my grave
So might a duteous daughter weep! God speed
Brave Malcolm to his father's land! they cried.
The ships beyond the promontory's point
Were anchored, and the tide was ebbing fast.
Then Ailric: Sire, not unforeseen by me
Was this sad day. Oh! King of Scotland, hear!
I was a brother of that holy house
Where Harold's bones are buried; from my vows
I was absolved, and followed—for I loved
His children—followed them through every fate.
My few gray hairs will soon descend in peace,
When I shall be forgotten; but till then,
My services, my last poor services,
To them I have devoted, for the sake
Of him, their father, and my king, to whom
All in this world I owed! Protect them, Lord,
And bless them, when the turf is on my head;
And, in their old age, may they sometimes think
Of Ailric, cold and shrouded in his grave,
When summer smiles! Sire, listen whilst I pray
One boon of thy compassion: not for me—
I reck not whether vengeance wake or sleep—
But for the safety of this innocent maid
I speak. South of the Humber, in a cave,
Concealed amidst the rocks and tangled brakes,
I have deposited some needful weeds
For this sad hour; for well, indeed, I knew,
If all should fail, this maiden's last resolve,
To kneel upon her father's grave, or die.
For this I have provided; but the time
Is precious, and the sun is westering slow;
The fierce eye of the lion may be turned
Upon this spot to-morrow! Adela,
Now hear your friend, your father! The fleet hour
Is passing, never to return: oh, seize
The instant! Thou, King Malcolm, grant my prayer!
If we embark, and leave the shores this night,
The voice of fame will bruit it far and wide,
That Harold's children fled with thee, and sought
A refuge in thy kingdom. None will know
Our destination. In thy boat conveyed,
We may be landed near the rocky cave;
The boat again ply to thy ships, and they

Plough homeward the north seas, whilst we are left
To fate. Again the pilot's voice was heard;
And, o'er the sand-hills, an approaching file
Of Norman soldiers, with projected spears,
Already seemed as rushing on their prey.
Then Ailric took the hand of Adela;
She and her brothers, and young Atheling,
And Scotland's king, are in one boat embarked.
Meantime the sun sets red, and twilight shades
The sinking hills. The solitary boat
Has reached the adverse shore.
Here, then, we part!
King Malcolm said; and every voice replied,
God speed brave Malcolm to his father's land!
Ailric, the brothers, and their sister, left
The boat; they stood upon the moonlit beach,
Still listening to the sounds, as they grew faint,
Of the receding oars, and watching still
If one white streak at distance, as they dipped,
Were seen, till all was solitude around.
Pensive, they sought a refuge for that night
In the bleak ocean-cave. The morning dawns;
The brothers have put off the plumes of war,
Dropping one tear upon the sword. Disguised
In garb to suit their fortunes, they appear
Like shipwrecked seamen of Armorica,
By a Franciscan hermit through the land
Led to St Alban's shrine, to offer vows,
Vows to the God who heard them in that hour
When all beside had perished in the storm.
Wrecked near his ocean-cave, an eremite
(So went the tale of their disastrous fate)
Sustained them, and now guides them through a land
Of strangers. That fair boy was wont to sing
Upon the mast, when the still ship went slow
Along the seas, in sunshine; and that garb
Conceals the lovely, light-haired Adela.
The cuckoo's note in the deep woods was heard
When forth, they fared. At many a convent gate
They stood and prayed for shelter, and their pace
Hastened, if, high amid the clouds, they marked
Some solitary castle lift its brow
Gray in the distance—hastened, so to reach,
Ere it grew dark, its hospitable towers.
There the lithe minstrel sung his roundelay:

Listen, lords and ladies bright!
I can sing of many a knight

Who fought in paynim lands afar;
Of Bevis, or of Iscapar.
I have tales of wandering maids,
And fairy elves in haunted glades,
Of phantom-troops that silent ride
By the moonlit forest's side.
I have songs (fair maidens, hear!)
To warn the lovelorn lady's ear.
The choice of all my treasures take,
And grant us food for pity's sake!

When tired, at noon, by the white waterfall,
In some romantic and secluded glen,
They sat, and heard the blackbird overhead
Singing, unseen, a song, such as they heard
In infancy. So every vernal morn
Brought with it scents of flowers, or songs of birds,
Mingled with many shapings of old things,
And days gone by. Then up again, to scale
The airy mountain, and behold the plain
Stretching below, and fading far away,
How beautiful; yet still to feel a tear
Starting, even when it shone most beautiful,
To think, Here, in the country of our birth,
No rest is ours!
On, to our father's grave!
So southward through the country they had passed
Now many days, and casual shelter found
In villages, or hermit's lonely cave,
Or castle, high embattled on the point
Of some steep mountain, or in convent walls;
For most with pity heard his song, and marked
The countenance of the wayfaring boy;
Or when the pale monk, with his folded hands
Upon his breast, prayed, For the love of God,
Pity the poor, give alms; and bade them speed!
And now, in distant light, the pinnacles
Of a gray fane appeared, whilst on the woods
Still evening shed its parting light. Oh, say,
Say, villager, what towers are those that rise
Eastward beyond the alders?
Know ye not,
He answered, Waltham Abbey? Harold there
Is buried—he who in the fight was slain
At Hastings! To the cheek of Adela
A deadly paleness came. On—let us on!
Faintly she cried, and held her brother's arm,
And hid her face a moment with her hand.

And now the massy portal's sculptured arch
Before them rose.
Say, porter, Ailric cried,
Poor mariners, wrecked on the northern shores,
Ask charity. Does aged Osgood live?
Tell him a poor Franciscan, wandering far,
And wearied, for the love of God would ask
His charity.
Osgood came slowly forth;
The light that touched the western turret fell
On his pale face. The pilgrim-father said:
I am your brother Ailric—look on me!
And these are Harold's children!
Whilst he spoke,
Godwin, advancing, with emotion cried,
We are his children! I am Godwin, this
Is Edmund, and, lo! poor and in disguise,
Our sister! We would kneel upon his grave—
Our father's!
Come yet nearer, Osgood said,
Yet nearer! and that instant Adela
Looked up, and wiping from her eyes a tear,
Have you forgotten Adela?
O God!
The old man trembling cried, ye are indeed
Our benefactor's children! Adela,
Edmund, brave Godwin! welcome to these walls—
Welcome, my old companion! and he fell
Upon the neck of Ailric, and both wept.
Then Osgood: Children of that honoured lord
Who gave us all, go near and bless his grave.
One parting sunbeam yet upon the floor
Rested—it passed away, and darker gloom
Was gathering in the aisles. Each footstep's sound
Was more distinctly heard, for all beside
Was silent. Slow along the glimmering fane
They passed, like shadows risen from the tombs.
The entrance-door was closed, lest aught intrude
Upon the sanctity of this sad hour.
The inner choir they enter, part in shade
And part in light, for now the rising moon
Began to glance upon the shrines, and tombs,
And pillars. Trembling through the windows high,
One beam, a moment, on that cold gray stone
Is flung—the word "Infelix" is scarce seen.
Behold his gravestone! Osgood said. Each eye
Was turned. A while intent they gazed, then knelt
Before the altar, on the marble stone!

No sound was heard through all the dim expanse
Of the vast building, none but of the air
That came in dying echoes up the aisle,
Like whispers heard at the confessional.
Thus Harold's children, hand in hand, knelt down—
Upon their father's grave knelt down, and prayed:
Have mercy on his soul—have mercy, Lord!
They knelt a lengthened space, and bowed their heads,
Some natural tears they shed, and crossed their breasts;
Then rising slowly up, looked round, and saw
A monk approaching near, unmarked before;
And in the further distance the tall form
As of a female. He who wore the hood
And habit of a monk approached and spoke:
Brothers! beloved sister! know ye not
These features?—and he raised his hood—Behold
Me—me, your brother Marcus! whom these weeds,
Since last we met, have hidden from the world:
Let me kneel with you here!
When Adela
Beheld him, she exclaimed, Oh! do we meet
Here, my lost brother, o'er a father's grave?
You live, restored a moment in this world,
To us as from the grave! And Godwin took
His hand, and said, My brother, tell us all;
How have you lived unknown? Oh! tell us all!
When in that grave our father, he replied,
Was laid, ye fled, and I in this sad land
Remained to cope with fortune. To these walls
I came, when Ailric, from his vows absolved,
With you was wandering. None my lineage knew,
Or name, but I some time had won regard
From the superior. Osgood knew me not,
For with Earl Edwin I had lived from youth.
To our superior thus I knelt and prayed:
Sir, I beseech you, for the love of God,
And of our Lady Mary, and St John,
You would receive me here to live and die
Among you. What most moved my heart to take
The vows was this, that here, from day to day,
From year to year, within the walls he raised,
I might behold my father's grave. This eve
I sat in the confessional, unseen,
When you approached. I scarce restrained the tear,
From many recollections, when I heard
A tale of sorrow and of sin. Come near,
Woman of woe!—and a wan woman stood
Before them, tall and stately; her dark eyes

Shone, as the uncertain lamp cast a brief glare,
And showed her neck, and raven hair, and lips
Moving. She spoke not, but advanced and knelt—
She, too—on Harold's grave; then prayed aloud,
O God, be merciful to him—and me!
Who art thou? Godwin cried.
Ah! know ye not
The wretched Editha? No children's love
Could equal mine! I trod among the dead—
Did I not, fathers?—trod among the dead
From corse to corse, or saw men's dying eyes
Fixed upon mine, and heard such groans as yet
Rive, with remembrance, my torn heart: I found
Him who rests here, where then he lay in blood!
When he was buried, I beheld the rites
At distance, and with broken heart retired
To the wild woods; there I have lived unseen
From that sad hour. Late when the tempest rocked,
At midnight, a proud soldier shelter sought
In my lone cell; 'twas when the storm was heard
Through the deep forest, and he too had knelt
At Harold's grave! Who was it? He! the king!
Say, fathers, was it not the hand of God
That led his footsteps there!—but has he learned
Humility? Oh! ask this bleeding land!
Last night a phantom came to me in dreams,
And a voice said, Come, visit my cold grave!
I came, by some mysterious impulse led;
I heard the even song, and when the sound
Had ceased, and all departed, save one monk,
Who stood and gazed upon this grave alone,
I prayed that he would hear me, at this hour,
Confess my secret sins, for my full heart
Was labouring. It was Harold's son who sat
In the confessional, to me unknown;
But all is now revealed—and lo! I stand
Before you!
As she spoke, a thrilling awe
Came to each heart: loftier she seemed to stand
In the dim moonlight; sorrowful, yet stern,
Her aspect; and her breast was seen to beat;
Her eyes were fixed, and shone with fearful light.
She raised her right hand, and her dark hair fell
Upon her neck, whilst all, scarce breathing, heard:
My spirit labours! she exclaimed. This night!
The tomb! the altar! Ha! the vision strains
My senses to oppression! Marked ye not
The trodden throne restored—the Saxon line

Of England's monarchs bursting through the gloom?
Lady, I look on thee! In distant years,
Even from the Northern throne which thou shalt share,
A warrior-monarch shall arise, whose arm,
In concert with this country, now bowed low,
Shall tear the eagle from a conqueror's grasp,
Far greater than this Norman!
Spare, O God!
My burning brain! Then, with a shriek, she fell,
Insensible, upon the Saxon's grave!
They bore her from the fane; and Godwin said,
Peace, peace be with her, now and evermore!
He, taking Marcus by the hand, Yet here
Thou shalt behold, behold from day to day,
This honoured grave! But where in the great world
Shall be thy place of rest, poor Adela?
O God, be ever with her! Marcus cried,
With her, and you, my brothers! Here we part,
Never to meet again. Whate'er your fate,
I shall remember with a brother's love,
And pray for you; but all my spirit rests
In other worlds—in worlds, oh! not like this!
Ye may return to this sad scene when I
Am dust and ashes; ye may yet return,
And visit this sad spot; perhaps when age
Or grief has brought such change of heart as now
I feel, then shall you look upon my grave,
And shed one tear for him whose latest prayer
Will be: Oh, bless you! bless my sister, Lord!
Then Adela, with lifted look composed:
Father, it is performed,—the duty vowed
When we returned to this devoted land,
The last sad duty of a daughter's love!
And now I go in peace—go to a world
Of sorrow, conscious that a father's voice
Speaks to my soul, and that thine eye, O God!
Whate'er the fortunes of our future days,
Is o'er us. Thou, direct our onward road!
O'er the last Saxon's grave, old Osgood raised
His hands and prayed:
Father of heaven and earth,
All is beneath Thine eye! 'Tis ours to bend
In silence. Children of misfortune, loved,
Revered—children of him who raised these roofs,
No home is found for you in this sad land;
And none, perhaps, may know the spot, or shed
A tear upon the earth where ye are laid!
So saying, on their heads he placed his hands,

And blessed them all; but, after pause, rejoined:
'Tis dangerous lingering here—the fire-eyed lynx
Would lap your blood! Westward, beyond the Lea,
There is a cell where ye may rest to-night.
The portal opened; on the battlements
The moonlight shone, silent and beautiful!
Before them lay their path through the wide world—
The nightingales were singing as they passed;
And, looking back upon the glimmering towers,
They, led by Ailric, and with thoughts on heaven,
Through the lone forest held their pensive way.

CONCLUSION

William, on his imperial throne, at York
Is seated, clad in steel, all but his face,
From casque to spur. His brow yet wears a frown,
And his eyes show the unextinguished fire
Of steadfast vengeance, as his inmost heart
Yet labours, like the ocean after storm.
His sword unsheathed appears, which none besides
Can wield; his sable beard, full and diffused,
Below the casque is spread; the lion ramps
Upon his mailed breast, engrailed with gold.
Behind him stand his barons, in dark file
Ranged, and each feature hid beneath the helms;
Spears, with escutcheoned banners on their points,
Above their heads are raised. Though all alike
Are cased in armour, know ye not that knight
Who next, behind the king, seems more intent
To listen, and a loftier stature bears?
'Tis bold Montgomerie; and he who kneels
Before the seat, his armour all with gules
Chequered, and chequered his small banneret,
Is Lord Fitzalain. William holds a scroll
In his right hand, and to Fitzalain speaks:
All these, the forfeited domains and land
Of Edwin and of Morcar, traitor-lords,
From Ely to the banks of Trent, I give
To thee and thine!
Fitzalian lowly knelt,
And kissed his iron hand; then slowly rose,
Whilst all the barons shouted, Live the king!

This is thy song, William the Conqueror,
The tale of Harold's children, and the grave

Of the last Saxon! The huge fortress frowns
Still on the Thames, where William's banner waved,
Though centuries year after year have passed,
As the stream flows for ever at its feet;
Harold, thy bones are scattered, and the tomb
That held them, where the Lea's lorn wave delayed,
Is seen no more; and the high fane, that heard
The Eleeson pealing for thy soul,
A fragment stands, and none will know the spot
Where those whom thou didst love in dust repose,
Thy children! But the tale may not be vain,
If haply it awake one duteous thought
Of filial tenderness.
That day of blood
Is passed, like a dark spectre: but it speaks
Even to the kingdoms of the earth:
Behold
The hand of God! From that dark day of blood,
When Vengeance triumphed, and the curfew knolled,
England, thy proud majestic policy
Slowly arose! Through centuries of shade
The pile august of British liberty
Towered, till behold it stand in clearer light
Illustrious. At its base, fell Tyranny
Gnashes his teeth, and drops the broken sword;
Whilst Freedom, Justice, to the cloudless skies
Uplift their radiant forms, and Fame aloft
Sounds o'er the subject seas, from east to west,
From north to south, her trumpet—England, live!
And rule, till waves and worlds shall be no more!

ILLUSTRATIONS FROM SPEED

"This victory thus obtained, Duke William wholly ascribed unto God, and by way of a solemne supplication or procession, gave him the thankes; and pitching for that night his pavilion among the bodies of the dead, the next day returned to Hastings, there to consult upon his great and most prosperously begun enterprise, giving first commandement for the buriall of his slain souldiers.

"But Morcar and Edwin, the unfortunate Queenes' brethren, by night escaping the battaile, came unto London, where, with the rest of the peeres, they beganne to lay the foundation of some fresh hopes; posting thence their messengers to raise a new supply, and to comfort the English (who, through all the land, were stricken into a fearefull astonishment with this unexpected newes) from a despairing feare, showing the chance of warre to be mutable, their number many and captaines sufficient to try another field. Alfred, Archbishop of Yorke, there present, and president of the assembly, stoutly and prudently gave his counsell forthwith to consecrate and crowne young Edgar Atheling (the true heire) for their king, to whom consented likewise both the sea-captaines and the Londoners. But the Earles of

Yorkeshire and Cheshire, Edwin and Morcar (whom this fearefull state of their country could not disswade from disloyaltie and ambition), plotting secretly to get the crown themselves, hindred that wise and noble designe. In which, while the sorrowfullQueene, their sister, was conueyed to Westchester, where, without state or title of a Queene, she led a solitary and quiet life.

"The mother of the slaine King did not so well moderate her womanly passions as to receive either comfort or counsell of her friends: the dead body of her sonneshee greatly desired, and to that end sent to the Conquerour two sage brethren of his Abbey at Waltham, who had accompanied him in his unfortunate expedition. Their names (as I finde them recorded in an olde manuscript) were Osegod and Ailric, whose message to the Conquerour, not without abundance of teares and feare, is there set downe in the tenour as followeth:

"'Noble Duke, and ere long to be a most great and mightie King, we thy most humble servants, destitute of all comfort (as we would we were also of life) are come to thee as sent from our brethren, whom this dead King hath placed in the monastery of Waltham, to attend the issue of this late dreadfullbattaile (wherein God favouring thy quarrell, he is now taken away and dead, which was our greatest comforter, and by whose onelybountifullgoodenesse we were relieved and maintained, whom hee had placed to serve God in that church). Wherefore wee most humbly request thee (now our dread lord) by that gracious favour which the Lord of lords hath showed unto thee, and for the reliefe of their soules, who in this quarrell have ended their dayes, that it may be lawfull for us by thy good leave safely to take and carry away with us the dead body of the King, the founder and builder of our church and monasterie; as also the bodies of such others as whom, for the reverence of him and for his sake, desired also to be buried with us, that the state of our church by their helpe strengthened, may be the stronger, and endure the firmer.' With whose so humble a request, and abundant teares, the victorious and worthy Duke moved, answered:

"'Your King (said he) unmindfull of his faith, although he have for the present endured the worthy punishment of his fault, yet hath he not therefore deserved to want the honour of a sepulchre or to lie unburied: were it but that he died a King, howsoever he came by the kingdom, my purpose is, for the reverence of him, and for the health of them who, having left their wives and possessions, have here in my quarrel lost their lives, to build here a church and a monastery with an hundred monkes in it, to pray for them for ever, and in the same church to bury your King above the rest, with all honour unto so great a prince, and for his sake to endow the same with great revenewes.'

"With which his courteous speech and promises, the two religious fathers, comforted and encouraged, again replied:

"'Not so, noble Duke, but grant this thy servants' most humble request, that we may, for God, by thy leave, receive the dead body of our founder, and to bury it in the place which himself in his lifetime appointed, that wee, cheered with the presence of his body, may thereof take comfort, and that his tombe may be unto our successors a perpetual monument of his remembrance.'

"The Duke, as he was of disposition gracious, and inclined to mercy, forthwith granted their desires, whereupon they drew out stores of gold to present him in way of gratulation, which he not only utterly refused, but also offered them plenty to supply whatsoever should be needfull for the pompe of his funerall, as also for their costs in travaile to and fro, giving strait commandments that none of his souldiers should persume to molest them in this businesse or in their returne. Then went they in haste to the quarry of the dead, but by no meanes could find the body of the King; for the countenances of all men greatly alter by death, but being maimed and imbrued with bloud, they are not known to be the men they were. As for his other regall ornaments which might have shewed him for their King, his dead corps was despoyled of them, either through the greedy desire of prey (as the manner of the field is) or to be the first bringer of such happy news, in hope of a princely reward, upon which purpose many times the body is both mangled and dismembred, and so was this King after his death by a base souldiergasht and hackt into the legge, whom Duke William rewarded for so unsouldier like a deed, cashiering him for ever out of his wages and warres. So that Harold, lying stript, wounded, bemangled, and goared in his bloud, could not be founde nor knowne till they sent for a woman named Editha (for her passing beautie surnamed Swan-shals, that is, Swan's-necke), whom hee entertained in secret love before he was King, who by some secret marks of his body, to her well knowne, found him out, and then put into a coffine, was by divers of the Norman nobilitiehonourably brought unto the place afterward called Battle Bridge, where it was met by the nobles of England, and, so conveyed to Waltham, was there solemnly and with great lamentation of his mother, royally interred, with this rude epitaph, well beseeming the time, though not the person.

"Goodwine, the eldest son of the King Harold, being growne to some ripenesse of years in ye life of his father, after his death and overthrow by the Conquerour, took his brother with him and flew over into Ireland, from whence he returned and landed in Somersetshire, slew Edmoth (a baron sometimes of his fathers) that encountered him, and taking great preyes in Devonshire and Cornwell, departed till the next yeare; when, comeing again, he fought with Beorn and Earle of Cornwall, and after retired into Ireland, and thence went into Denmarke to King Swayn, his cosen-german, where he spent the rest of his life.

"Edmund, the second sonne to King Harold, went with his brother into Ireland, returned with him into England, and was at the slaughter and overthrow of Edmoth and his power in Somersetshire, at the spoyles committed in Cornwall and Devonshire, at the conflict with the Cornish Earle Beorn, passed, repassed with him in all his voyages, invasions, and warres, by sea and by land, in England and Ireland; and at the last departed with him from Ireland to Denmarke, tooke part with him of all pleasure and calamitie whatsoever, and attending and depending wholly upon him, lived and died with him in that country.

"Magnus, the third sonne of the King Harold, went with his brothers into Ireland, and returned with them the first time into England, and is never after that mentioned amongst them, nor elsewhere, unlesse (as some conjecture) he be that Magnus, who, seeing the mutability of humane affaires, became an anchoret, whose epitaph, pointing to his Danish originall, the learned Clarenciaux discovered in a little desolate church at Lewes, in Sussex, where, in the gaping chinks of an arch in the wall, in a rude and over worne character, certain old imperfect verses were found."

A daughter, whose name is not known, left England with her brothers, and sought refuge with them in Denmark.

Speed quotes Saxo Grammaticus, who says, "She afterwards married Waldemar, King of Russia." To this daughter I have given the name and character assigned to her in the poem.

William Lisle Bowles was born on 24th September 1762 at King's Sutton in Northamptonshire.

His great-grandfather, grandfather and his father, William Thomas Bowles, had all been parish priests and inevitably Bowles would join their line.

At the age of 14 he entered Winchester College, where the headmaster was Dr Joseph Warton (a minor poet, his most notable piece is The Enthusiast, 1744. In 1755, he taught at Winchester and from 1766 to 1793 was headmaster. His career as a critic was illustrious. He produced editions of poets such as Virgil as well as several English poets).

In 1789 Bowles published, a small quarto volume, Fourteen Sonnets, which was received with extraordinary praise, not only by the general public, but by such revered poets as Samuel Taylor Coleridge and Wordsworth.

The Sonnets were a return to an older and purer poetic style, and by their grace of expression, lyrical versification, tender tone of feeling and vivid appreciation of the wonder and beauty of nature, stood out in marked contrast to the elaborate works which then formed the bulk of English poetry.

Bowles said "Poetic trifles from solitary rambles whilst chewing the cud of sweet and bitter fancy, written from memory, confined to fourteen lines, this seemed best adapted to the unity of sentiment, the verse flowed in unpremeditated harmony as my ear directed but are far from being mere elegiac couplets".

The young Samuel Taylor Coleridge felt obliged to record his debt of gratitude to Bowles: "My obligations to Mr. Bowles were indeed important, and for radical good. At a very premature age, ... I had bewildered myself in metaphysicks, and in theological controversy. Nothing else pleased me. Poetry ... became insipid to me.... This preposterous pursuit was, beyond doubt, injurious both to my natural powers, and to the progress of my education.... But from this I was auspiciously withdrawn, chiefly by the genial influence of a style of poetry, so tender and yet so manly, so natural and real, and yet so dignified and harmonious, as the sonnets &c. of Mr. Bowles!"

In 1781 Bowles left as captain of Winchester school, and proceeded to Trinity College, Oxford, after winning a scholarship. Two years later he won the Chancellor's prize for Latin verse. It was now evident that the Church and poetry were to be his two callings.

After receiving his degree at Oxford, Bowles now began his career in service to the Church of England. In 1792, after serving as curate in Donhead St Andrew, Bowles was appointed vicar of Chicklade in Wiltshire.

Five years later, in 1797, he received the vicarage of Dumbleton in Gloucestershire, and in 1804 became vicar of Bremhill in Wiltshire, where he wrote the poem seen on Maud Heath's statue. In the same year his bishop, John Douglas, collated him to a prebendal stall in Salisbury Cathedral.

In 1818 Bowles was made chaplain to the Prince Regent, and in 1828 he was elected residentiary canon of Salisbury.

His years of service perhaps diminished both his stature as a poet and certainly the way he was viewed. For much of his career Bowles was seen as rather soft when set against his contemporaries but in the end his ability as a poet was enshrined, after a long and ferocious attack against him, by the principles he so eloquently wrote about and adhered too.

It is as well to remember that when critics suggest that compared to other poets his longer works were not to the standard that the competition achieved, that this era is perhaps without poetic equal. Set against Byron, Shelley, Keats, Wordsworth and other great luminaries of the era it is perhaps difficult to see his works in isolation for their own value.

The longer poems published by Bowles are distinguished by purity of imagination, cultured and graceful diction, and a great thoughtfulness of feeling. Among them were The Spirit of Discovery (1804), which alas was so mercilessly ridiculed by Byron; The Missionary (1813); The Grave of the Last Saxon (1822); and St John in Patmos (1833).

In 1806 he published an edition of Alexander Pope's works with notes and an essay, in which he laid down certain canons as to poetic imagery which, subject to some modification, were later accepted, but received at the time with strong opposition by admirers of Pope.

Bowles restated his views in 1819, in The Invariable Principles of Poetry. The controversy brought into sharp contrast the opposing views of poetry, which may be thought of as being either the natural or the artificial.

In personality and nature Bowles was said to be an amiable, absent-minded, but rather eccentric man. His poems speak warmly of a refinement of feeling, tenderness, and pensive thought, but are lacking in power and passion. But that should not diminish their value or appreciation to us.

Bowles maintained that images drawn from nature are poetically finer than those drawn from art; and that in the highest kinds of poetry the themes or passions handled should be of the general or elemental kind, and not the transient manners of any society. These positions were attacked by Byron, Thomas Campbell, William Roscoe and others, and for a time Bowles had to fight his corner on his own. Soon however, William Hazlitt and the Blackwood critics came to his assistance, and on the whole Bowles had reason to congratulate himself on having established certain principles which might serve as the basis of a true method of poetical criticism, and of having inaugurated, both by precept and by example, a new era in English poetry.

As well as his poetry Bowles was also responsible for writing a Life of Bishop Ken (in two volumes, 1830–1831), Coombe Ellen and St. Michael's Mount (1798), The Battle of the Nile (1799), and The Sorrows of Switzerland (1801).

Bowles also enjoyed considerable reputation as an antiquary and his principal work in that field was Hermes Britannicus (1828).

William Lisle Bowles died on April 7th, 1850 at the age of 87.